QUICK GUIDE TO
FANTASY
BASEBALL

by Bo Mitchell

D1518847

BrightPoint Press

San Diego, CA

BrightPoint Press

© 2021 BrightPoint Press
an imprint of ReferencePoint Press, Inc.
Printed in the United States

For more information, contact:
BrightPoint Press
PO Box 27779
San Diego, CA 92198
www.BrightPointPress.com

LIBRARY OF CONGRESS CATALOGING-IN-PUBLICATION DATA

Names: Mitchell, Bo, author.
Title: Quick guide to fantasy baseball / by Bo Mitchell.
Description: San Diego, CA : ReferencePoint Press, [2021] | Series: Quick guide to fantasy
    sports | Includes bibliographical references and index. | Audience: Grades 10-12
Identifiers: LCCN 2020002424 (print) | LCCN 2020002425 (eBook) | ISBN 9781678200008
    (Hardcover) | ISBN 9781678200015 (eBook)
Subjects: LCSH: Fantasy baseball (Game)--Juvenile literature.
Classification: LCC GV1202.F33 M38 2021 (print) | LCC GV1202.F33 (eBook) | DDC
    794.9/357--dc23
LC record available at https://lccn.loc.gov/2020002424
LC eBook record available at https://lccn.loc.gov/2020002425

CONTENTS

AT A GLANCE

- Fantasy baseball is a fun way for MLB fans to learn more about the game.

- Participants earn points based on the statistics of MLB players.

- League commissioners organize the league and set it up online.

- Leagues establish clear rules before the season begins. Many customize their rules.

- Many websites host fantasy baseball leagues.

- There are two popular forms of fantasy baseball. They are Rotisserie and head-to-head.

- Participants use a draft or an auction to build their teams.

- Sources and tools to help manage teams are easy to find, including websites, magazines, TV shows, radio shows, and podcasts.

- Adding free agents and making trades improves a team.

- Participants set their lineups every week of the season.

- Owners should never give up on their teams. Stay active and keep trying.

JOINING A LEAGUE

"I can't wait to go to the home opener, Dad!" Holden said. "You got those good seats on the third-base line, right?"

"That's right," his dad said. "Bring your glove. Maybe you can catch a foul ball."

Holden loves baseball. He has been playing since he was old enough to hold

Any baseball fan can join a fantasy league.

a bat. He keeps baseball cards all over his

bedroom. He knows a lot about the players.

Talking about baseball is one of his favorite

things to do.

Most leagues are made of people who know each other. Friends, family, or teammates are all good people to invite to play.

"Dad, I'm playing fantasy baseball again this year," Holden said as he sat down at the kitchen table. "I finished in third place last year. I had Mike Trout, Max Kepler, and

Justin Verlander. I really want to win this season. I need to try to get better pitchers on my team. Javy is getting a league together. You remember him from my baseball team, right?"

"I sure do," said his dad. "Who else is in Javy's league?"

"Well, a few other guys from the team are going to play. So is Javy's sister Maria and her friend Omar," said Holden. "We almost have enough people. Some of them have never played fantasy baseball before."

"You should ask your sister to play," his dad said. "Kourtney really knows her stuff."

"That's a good idea," Holden replied. "She hasn't played fantasy baseball before. But she's a big fan of baseball. She'll figure it out quickly."

FANTASY BASEBALL IS FOR EVERYONE

Fantasy baseball is for anyone who enjoys the sport. It's also a great way to learn more about baseball. Setting up a league is easy. It can be done online. Fans of any age can pick it up quickly. Participants don't need to know all of the stats in order to play. Owners can manage their teams using a variety of sources and tools. All it takes is an interest in baseball.

Knowing stats is helpful, but participants can learn along the way.

CHAPTER ONE

WHAT IS FANTASY BASEBALL?

Baseball uses many statistics. Fans often know common stats. Some fans keep track of batting averages. Even new fans know about home runs and strikeouts. Statistics shape MLB games. They also determine the success of fantasy baseball. Fantasy baseball is a game where

Fantasy baseball uses MLB stats to determine how well fantasy teams do.

League size affects how much talent is available per team.

fans create teams of MLB players. These

teams compete against each other. The

team with the best stats wins.

FORMING A FANTASY BASEBALL LEAGUE

The first step in starting a league is finding people to play. An MLB season lasts six months. However, finding fans to participate shouldn't be tough. Leagues generally have ten or twelve teams. Fewer teams means every team is filled with star players. More than that and there might not be enough good players for everyone. Fantasy baseball becomes challenging with more teams.

Fantasy baseball participants are called "owners." Some people call them "managers." Owners run the team.

They select players. They decide who plays every week. A group of owners forms a league.

Most owners begin to follow every MLB team. It becomes important to know who is doing well. Beating other owners is fun. Winners get all the bragging rights.

CO-OWNING A TEAM

Following baseball all season can seem like too much. However, there's another solution. Sometimes people co-own a team. It cuts down on the work. There are a lot of MLB players. Having two people to scout players and set **lineups** can make things easier. Finding the right friend to help can be tricky. But a good partner can lead to success.

Most leagues last one MLB season. They start in March and go through September. The goal is to have the best team at the end of the season. To determine this, MLB player stats are used. Players have good and bad games. They have good and bad stats. Hitters get home runs and groundouts. Pitchers get wins and losses. Successful owners predict who the best players will be.

THE STATS THAT MATTER

Owners don't need to know every stat to play. Knowledge of basic baseball statistics is enough. Stats determine how well a fantasy team is doing.

5x5 leagues use ten categories. There are five hitting and five pitching categories. "You'll notice some balance," says Eno Sarris of Fangraphs.com. "Power players dominate two offensive categories while

CUSTOMIZABLE STATS

A variety of statistics can be used in fantasy. Some leagues choose to use different stats. Total bases (TB), on-base percentage (OBP), or on-base plus slugging (OPS) can replace batting average. Quality starts (QS) can replace wins. Strikeouts per nine innings (K/9) can replace strikeouts. Leagues can decide to make these changes.

speedier on-base guys have a chance to help in three. Starting pitchers are needed for strikeouts and wins, but you still have to have good relievers to help keep the ratios down and get saves."[1]

Some leagues use a 4x4 format for scoring. They use four pitching categories and four hitting categories. These leagues don't typically use strikeouts and runs.

ROTISSERIE LEAGUES

Rotisserie and head-to-head are two popular league formats. Rotisserie baseball was invented in 1980 by writer Dan Okrent. Okrent and other fans met at a restaurant in

New York City. It was called La Rotisserie. This is where this format gets its name. Rotisserie baseball is also called "roto." In this form, teams are ranked in each stat category. For example, the team with the most home runs gets points equal to the number of teams in the league. They get ten points if there are ten teams in the league. The second-place team would get nine points. This would continue for all the teams. The team with the fewest home runs gets one point.

This is done for all stats. Teams earn points based on where they rank

Players in a roto league want to earn the most points in as many categories as possible.

in each category. If a league has ten

categories and ten teams, the highest

possible score is one hundred points. All

of a team's points are added together. A

running total is kept. The points are used to

KEEPER AND DYNASTY LEAGUES

Keeper and dynasty leagues last several seasons. Owners stay in these leagues several years. Some players can be kept from one season to the next. In dynasty leagues, every player is allowed to be held for as long as the owner wants. Minor league players are even eligible to be **drafted** in dynasty leagues. They cannot score points until they reach the majors. But it is one way to draft young talent early. There's more strategy involved in keeper and dynasty formats. Younger players become more valuable.

establish rankings. Teams can see how they compare to others. The rankings are kept all season long. The team in the lead at the end of the season wins.

HEAD-TO-HEAD LEAGUES

Head-to-head leagues use the same statistics as roto. However, scoring is different. Roto compares teams all season. In head-to-head leagues, each team competes against another each week. The league needs an even number of teams. The team with the most points wins. Every stat has a point value. Leagues use counting stats like hits, home runs, and wins. Stats like ERA and batting average are sometimes replaced. A single might be worth one point. A home run could be worth four. Mike Trout's forty-five home runs in 2019 are worth 180 points in this system. That's just home runs. Trout hit twenty-seven doubles. Those earned another fifty-four points. Scoring can be done in different ways. The idea remains the same. Two teams face off. This continues all season. Wins and losses are determined weekly.

The top teams go to the playoffs. Many leagues start their playoffs in early

No matter what format a league uses, owners want to win.

September. These matchups are during the final month of the MLB season. The results determine the champion.

Which is better? Roto or head-to-head? "It really depends on what you enjoy about the game," says ESPN.com's Rick Paulas. "If you're into the thrill of a walk-off home run victory. . . then you won't mind giving up the more accurate method of scoring for a head-to-head playoff system."[2]

Teams in head-to-head leagues are actively trying to defeat a single opponent.

FANTASY STATS

Fantasy baseball traditionally uses ten stat categories. Each of these categories covers a variety of player strengths. A player who is weak in one or two categories can earn points in the others.

HITTING STATS

Batting Average	AVG	Measures a player's hitting ability by dividing their hits by their total at-bats
Home Runs	HR	The batter hits the ball and is able to score during the same play
Runs Batted In	RBI	A run that scores as the result of a batter's actions
Runs	R	When a player scores for his team
Stolen Bases	SB	When a player on base runs to the next base before the ball has been hit

PITCHING STATS

Wins	W	Given to the pitcher from the winning team who was in the lineup when the go-ahead run scored
Saves	SV	Given to a relief pitcher who closes out a victory
Strikeouts	K	Three strikes against a batter
Earned-Run Average	ERA	The number of earned runs a pitcher allows per nine innings
Walks Plus Hits Per Innings Pitched	WHIP	The walks and hits allowed divided by the number of innings pitched

CHAPTER TWO

HOW DO FANTASY BASEBALL LEAGUES GET STARTED?

A league needs someone in charge. That person is the **commissioner**. Commissioners hold the draft. They set up the league website. They review and approve trades.

There are many things a league must agree on, including rules.

George Kurtz of Fantasydata.com

suggests having a league constitution.

"This will cover any problems that come

up during the season. This way you don't

have to worry about a commissioner

Fantasy baseball was popularized by the media in the 1980s.

making up the rules as he or she goes

along."[3] The constitution should be on the

league's website.

RUNNING A LEAGUE ONLINE

Fantasy football existed almost twenty

years before fantasy baseball. But fantasy

baseball helped popularize fantasy sports.

Many early participants were in the media.

In 1981, MLB players went on strike. Many

sportswriters covered fantasy leagues.

These teams had been drafted before

the strike. They continued to write about

fantasy until play resumed. Fans began

to participate.

In fantasy football, scoring only needs to be done once a week. Since MLB games are daily, standings change constantly. It was difficult for early leagues to keep up. Standings were only updated periodically. It was too much work to update daily. Early commissioners had to do it by hand. That's no longer the case. Leagues are now online. Statistics are updated in real time.

ROSTER AND LINEUP REQUIREMENTS

A league must decide what format they want to play. They must agree on stat categories. Other rules are needed. The league must decide each team's size.

Most fantasy lineups are much larger than an MLB lineup.

Most have twenty to thirty roster spots.

Keeper and dynasty leagues often have

more. Team size depends on the number of

bench players allowed. Owners set a lineup

each week. They fill every position.

Nonstarting players are on the bench. Stats

only count for the active lineup. Lineups

can change weekly. Some leagues allow

daily changes.

Typically, a starting lineup has eight to ten

pitchers. It has ten or more hitters. Teams

need one hitter for each infield spot. These

spots are catcher, first base, second base,

third base, and shortstop. They need three

The Los Angeles Angels signed Japanese baseball star Shohei Ohtani in 2018. He was called the "Japanese Babe Ruth." Ohtani is both a hitter and a pitcher. The Angels used Ohtani as both. This caused a problem for fantasy. Leagues must decide if he can be used as a hitter, pitcher, or both. This affects how owners can assign him.

outfielders. Some leagues allow more. Most leagues require a utility hitter. They can be any position player or designated hitter. Many leagues also allow one additional middle infielder. This would be a shortstop or second baseman. They also allow an

extra corner infielder. This would be a first
or third baseman.

Bench players round out the roster.
Some leagues only have five bench spots.
Others allow ten. Some have even more.
Each league decides for itself. Once a
league settles on lineup requirements and
roster sizes, it needs to define how players
qualify for positions.

POSITION ELIGIBILITY

Baseball players can play multiple positions.
Leagues define how players are assigned
positions. This is called **position eligibility**.
Certain positions like shortstop and second

Many MLB players play multiple positions. This can make them more valuable.

base often have better fielders than hitters.

Sometimes a great hitter is moved from

his normal spot. If he plays part of a game

somewhere new, should owners be allowed

to use him there? That creates an unfair

advantage. For example, Cubs slugger

Shohei Ohtani was signed by the Angels as both a hitter and pitcher. This gave fantasy owners more flexibility on how to use him.

Anthony Rizzo moved from first to second base for ten games in 2017. Should fantasy teams have been allowed to use him as a second baseman? How about when Rizzo played one game at second in 2018?

Leagues need limits. Typically, a player needs to have played a certain number of games at a position the prior season. Each league needs to decide how many games. "Some require that five games be played at a position the previous season, while some require 10 or 20," points out Michael Florio of RotoExperts.com. "Knowing this will not only give you lineup flexibility during the season, but in the draft as well."[4] MLB players can switch positions midseason. Offseason changes are also common. Owners want them to play at their new positions. Normally, leagues allow a

AUCTIONS

Owners can "buy" players instead of drafting them. This is an auction. It's an alternative to a draft. Each owner gets the same imaginary amount of money to spend. Owners take turns nominating players to bid on. The player goes to the highest bidder. The money must last the entire auction. Get a friend not in the league to be the auctioneer. That keeps things fair.

player to be in a new position after at least ten games.

Players that play a lot of games at multiple positions have increased value. Two examples of this are Max Muncy and Eduardo Escobar. They both play several infield positions.

THE DRAFT

Most leagues hold a draft before the start of the MLB season. Each team selects its players. Owners take turns picking players. They pick until every team is full. Draft order can be determined any way the league wants. The length of the draft depends on team size. If each team needs twenty-five players, the draft lasts twenty-five rounds. It can take several hours.

A draft should have an order so each team gets a fair chance to pick. However, drafts don't have to use the same order each round. Reversing the order every round is common. This is fairer than picking Team One to Team Ten every round. This back-and-forth order is referred to as a "snake" or "serpentine" draft. Drafts can be done online. Some leagues draft in person. Draft day is the biggest day for fantasy baseball. Some leagues throw parties.

Any draft style works as long as the league agrees on it.

CHAPTER THREE

HOW DO FANTASY BASEBALL OWNERS PREPARE?

Winning requires luck. Players get injured or have slumps. Sometimes a team does well. However, their opponent may do better. Preparation reduces the impact of bad luck. Owners must get ready

Preparation helps set owners up for the best season possible.

for draft day. Good owners know which

players to select and when. They have

a plan.

There are many resources online to help owners plan for the season.

STUDY THE STATISTICS

Owners get information from stats. There are many statistics. However, owners only need stats their league uses. Finding them is easy. Baseball websites and magazines often include past stats. Who did well in past seasons? Owners should check the categories their league uses. However, player stats change from season to season. Owners must figure out how they will change. They do research. Fortunately, great resources are easy to find.

ANALYSIS AND TOOLS

Analyzing stats is just as important as finding them. Owners can get help breaking down the numbers. Fantasy baseball television shows, radio shows, and podcasts are great sources. These also have current baseball news. Players sign with new teams, get traded, and are injured. These changes can affect player values. Most fantasy resources include articles on sleepers. These are players that might be undervalued. There's also analysis on overhyped players. These are referred to as busts. It's helpful to get different opinions.

Looking at mock drafts is helpful. Taking part is even better. Owners can get a good idea of when players are being selected. Picking from various spots in the draft order is useful. Take part in a handful of mock drafts to get a good feel. Practice picking late when players like Mike Trout, Christian Yelich, and Cody Bellinger are no longer available. Which players are the best picks at the ninth or tenth spots? It's great practice for the real draft. Many fantasy websites offer free mock drafts.

Owners should look into rookies and minor league players. MLB teams call up players from the minors throughout the season. Knowing the best ones is useful.

Many resources feature **mock drafts**. These are conducted by experts.

Owners want to make sure they don't draft
lower-ranked players too early.

Mock drafts show how actual drafts might unfold. Owners can learn a lot. It's helpful to see when certain players get drafted. They show how early or late positions are drafted.

HAVING A SUCCESSFUL DRAFT

The most important draft tool is a **cheat sheet**. A cheat sheet is a list of players. They are sorted by position. Players are ranked from best to worst. Experts provide their rankings. Cheat sheets are in magazines and online. Owners should study them. They should have one with them while drafting. Owners mark off drafted players. This makes it easy to tell who is still available. Cheat sheets exist for different scoring systems. Some are for 5x5 leagues. Others are for 4x4 leagues. Some are designed for head-to-head formats. There are also cheat sheets for keeper and dynasty leagues. Owners should find the right one.

During the draft, owners must pay attention to which positions they have already filled. They should focus on positions they still need. If drafting online, the website will track this. Above all, owners need to like their teams. Everyone should draft some of their favorites. "Research

When drafting, owners might consider choosing a favorite player even if they might not be the strongest in a category.

Both starters and closers are important for a team to score well in pitching categories.

well and prepare for your draft, but at the end of the day the most important thing to do is to follow your gut," says Matt Cott of RotoAnalysis. "Go with your guys because it's way better to lose with your guys then lose without your guys and having them all go off."[5]

POSITION SCARCITY

Be mindful of **position scarcity**. This is the number of quality players at a position. There used to be more good hitters among outfielders, first basemen, and third basemen. Catchers, second basemen, and shortstops are known for their gloves. However, the gap isn't what it used to be. Talented hitters can be found at every position. AJ Mass of ESPN.com keeps position scarcity in mind "to use as a tiebreaker of sorts when debating between two or more players of relatively equal value."[6] This is helpful when deciding

CLOSERS

Closers are pitchers that get the final outs of a game. They earn saves. Most teams have one closer like Kenley Jansen or Josh Hader. Some use more. Owners need saves. But most closers only help with saves. They don't pitch enough to help with strikeouts, ERA, or WHIP. Beware of taking a closer too early in the draft.

between a catcher like Mitch Garver and an

outfielder with similar hitting stats like Austin

Meadows. The catcher might be better.

Fewer good ones are available.

CHAPTER FOUR

HOW DO OWNERS MANAGE A TEAM?

An owner's job doesn't end when the draft ends. It's just beginning. Owners manage their teams all season. Players go in slumps. They get injured. Stars emerge. Owners must adjust to

Owners should look for ways to improve their teams all season.

stay competitive. The most important job is
to set their starting lineup.

SETTING A LINEUP

A lineup can make the difference between
winning and losing. Success isn't only

STARTING PITCHERS

Knowing which pitchers are scheduled to start is important when setting a lineup. Some pitchers start twice in a week. Most websites have probable pitcher information. Owners usually start their best pitchers. However, sometimes owners must decide between two pitchers of similar ability. Using the pitcher with two scheduled starts is sometimes the right call. They have twice as many opportunities to help score.

about the players on the roster. Knowing who should play each week is key. Websites make it easy to adjust lineups.

Some lineup decisions are obvious. Owners should always start star players like Alex Bregman and Anthony Rendon. Teams rarely have stars at every position, though. Owners need to look at their options. There are several factors to consider. Is someone playing well? Or are they struggling? How many games will they play that week? Some players are better at home than on the road. Others help boost a specific stat. Maybe a team wants more stolen bases.

Owners should adjust their lineups based on player performance.

It makes sense to start someone that steals more bases. Owners should use stats to make decisions. Not all lineup decisions work out. Even the best players have bad games. Making informed lineup decisions leads to the most success.

INJURED LIST

Injured players can be out for a while. Their team needs to make a change. MLB teams can place hurt players on their Injured List. Another player fills in. MLB teams usually call up a minor leaguer. Injuries change fantasy lineups, too. Most leagues have spots to store injured players. These injury spots don't count toward the active roster. A fantasy team can replace injured players.

ROSTER CHANGES

MLB players who aren't on a fantasy team are called **free agents**. They are available to be added. Some are used to fill in for an injured player. Otherwise, a player needs to be dropped if someone is added. Owners should stay alert for chances to improve. "Keep an eye out for notes on your players and check any news that comes through the pipeline," stresses Ghoji Blackburn of SB Nation. "Also, be proactive in researching the free agents in your league.

Adding free agents is not a permanent decision. Those who don't work out can be dropped and replaced later.

Don't be afraid to propose a trade to another owner. The worst they can say is no.

It is beneficial to know who is available in case you need to make a pick up."[7]

There are more players to follow in fantasy baseball than in other fantasy sports. The rosters and lineups are much larger.

Leagues have rules about adding free agents. They are referred to as **waiver rules**. Sometimes teams in last place are first to add free agents. Those doing well pick last. Other leagues allow players to be added on a first-come, first-served basis.

Another popular system is an in-season auction. This can be done on most websites. Each team has a free agent acquisition budget (FAAB). FAAB is fake money that owners can spend on free agents. Owners bid on a player. Nobody knows what the other owners bid. The bids are submitted by a certain day of the week. This day is typically a weekend. The winning bids are revealed. Then the rosters are changed. If an owner didn't win the bid, they can add other players. This enables every team to have a full roster each week.

FANTASY BASEBALL TRADES

Sometimes owners don't like the free agents in their league. It might seem like all the good players are on other teams. "There are always ways to improve your fantasy baseball team," says Eric Karabell of ESPN.com. "Never be afraid to take some chances not only on draft day, but also with a free agent or in a trade."[8] Making trades is a great way to change a fantasy roster.

Trades are less common than adding free agents. Negotiating trades is part of the fun. An owner can usually get a better player by making a trade. Remember though, a valuable player needs to be given up

Staying active is a lot of work, but it will pay off if the team does well.

in order to get one in return. Nobody's going to trade a star like Francisco Lindor for a bench player. Trades don't have to be limited to one player from each team. Several players can be traded in one deal. In keeper and dynasty leagues, owners can include future draft picks. Most leagues have a trade deadline late in the season.

No trades can be done after it. This keeps teams from affecting the playoffs.

IT'S A LONG SEASON

The MLB season is 162 games long. There are MLB games seven days a week for six months. Fantasy owners need to be up to the challenge. Staying active helps a team succeed. It is also good for the league. This is important late in the season. Some teams are trying to reach the playoffs. Keep setting good lineups. Keep making free agent moves. Owners should always try their best throughout the season. Have fun and good luck!

GLOSSARY

cheat sheet

A ranking of players, sorted by position, to help owners in fantasy baseball drafts.

draft

The most popular way for owners to select players for their fantasy baseball teams.

free agents

MLB players who aren't on fantasy baseball teams in a league.

mock draft

A practice draft used as a tool to help owners prepare for their real draft.

position eligibility

Rules about which players can be used for different positions in a fantasy baseball lineup.

position scarcity

The amount of talent at a position compared with the amount of talent at other positions.

waiver rules

Guidelines for picking up and dropping players from a fantasy team.

SOURCE NOTES

CHAPTER ONE: WHAT IS FANTASY BASEBALL?

1. Eno Sarris, "The Best Settings for Your Fantasy Baseball League," *Fangraphs*, February 3, 2014. fantasy.fangraphs.com.

2. Rick Paulas, "Fantasy World: The Debate Begins," *ESPN.com*, February 18, 2009. www.espn.com.

CHAPTER TWO: HOW DO FANTASY BASEBALL LEAGUES GET STARTED?

3. George Kurtz, "7 Ways to Make Your Fantasy Baseball League Better," *Fantasy Data*, March 15, 2019. fantasydata.com.

4. "Drafting Multi-Position Eligible Players Gives You an Edge," *RotoExperts*, March 10, 2017. rotoexperts.com.

CHAPTER THREE: HOW DO FANTASY BASEBALL OWNERS PREPARE?

5. Matt Cott, Matthew Schwimmer, and Moe Koltun, "Fantasy Baseball Edge: Three Big Tips for Winning Your League," *CBS Philly*, March 13, 2013. philadelphia.cbslocal.com

6. "How to Handle Position Scarcity," *ESPN. com*, February 26, 2018. www.espn.com.

CHAPTER FOUR: HOW DO OWNERS MANAGE A TEAM?

7. Ghoji Blackburn, "Fantasy Baseball Draft Strategies," *Fake Team* (blog), *SB Nation*, March 21, 2017. www.faketeams.com.

8. "Fantasy Baseball 101: How to Play Our Most Popular Game Formats," *ESPN.com*, February 26, 2018. www.espn.com.

FOR FURTHER RESEARCH

BOOKS

John Allen, *The Science and Technology of Baseball*. San Diego, CA: ReferencePoint Press, 2020.

Marty Gitlin, *Baseball: Underdog Stories*. Minneapolis, MN: Abdo Publishing, 2019.

Allan Morey, *Fantasy Baseball Math: Using Stats to Score Big in Your League*. North Mankato, MN: Capstone Press. 2017.

INTERNET SOURCES

Andrew Gould, "How to Play Fantasy Baseball: Tips and Advice for Your MLB League," *Bleacher Report*, March 12, 2019. www.bleacherreport.com.

"Fantasy Baseball Cheat Sheet Central," *ESPN.com*, February 21, 2018. www.espn.com.

"Fantasy Baseball Draft Simulator," *FantasyPros*, n.d. draftwizard.fantasypros.com.

WEBSITES

ESPN.com
www.espn.com/fantasy/baseball

ESPN.com features fantasy sports information, articles by experts, cheat sheets, mock drafts, and a league hosting service.

Rotoworld
www.rotoworld.com/sports/mlb/baseball

Rotoworld is a fantasy sports information website. It provides breaking MLB news and fantasy baseball analysis.

Yahoo! Fantasy
baseball.fantasysports.yahoo.com

Yahoo has a popular fantasy baseball league hosting service as well as breaking news and analysis from around the major leagues.

INDEX

IMAGE CREDITS

ABOUT THE AUTHOR

Bo Mitchell has lived in Minnesota his entire life and graduated from the University of Minnesota in Minneapolis. He started playing fantasy baseball in 1988 and then started writing about sports professionally in 1993. He has authored several educational books about sports and has written about sports for magazines and many websites. Most recently, Bo has worked as a sports statistics research analyst for many years.